# THE AGE OF KRYPTON

# The Age of Krypton

poems by

## Carol J. Pierman

Carnegie Mellon University Press
Pittsburgh 1989

# ACKNOWLEDGMENTS

Acknowledgment is made to editors of the following magazines in which many of these poems first appeared:

*Ascent*: Nova
*Carolina Quarterly*: The Changelings, Eight Cows
*Centennial Review*: The Incredible Journey, Eight Cows
*Cincinnati Poetry Review*: Absent, The Appointment,
          Polio Summer, Public Health, Seen in the
          Blue/Fluttering Like an Old Movie
*Florida Review*: The Mecca Court & Grill
*Lake Shore Review*: Hearing Harry Say
*Open Places*: Fish Hands, Les Deux Paulettes
*Painted Bride Quarterly*: Beginning Perspective
*River Styx*: Sincere
*Rusty Edge Review*: Gum for Breakfast
*Three Rivers Poetry Journal*: Cinema Vérité, How We Learned
          About Friction, Le Côte d'Azur, Rocket Athletic
          Boosters, The Winding Sheet

*American Anthology of Magazine Verse*: Reprint of "The
Word" in its 1985 edition

The Illinois Arts Council provided support for this book
through Artists' Fellowships in 1985 and 1986.

The publication of this book is supported by grants from the
National Endowment for the Arts in Washington, D. C., a
Federal agency, and by the Pennsylvania Council on the Arts.

Library of Congress Catalog Card Number 88-70389
ISBN 0-88748-075-6 Pbk.

# CONTENTS

## PART IV — THE AGE OF KRYPTON

For James and Ellin Pierman, Shelley and Jamie Pierman,
and for Sandy Huss

# PART ONE — A MODERN WORLD

# HOW WE LEARNED ABOUT FRICTION

A pink eraser rubbed to shreds
or chewed until our teeth got hot.
A sandy taste. The teacher said,
Brush your erasures from your desks.

We rubbed like insects sang,
wiping out the lopsided cow,
the silent letter, the incorrect
capital for Idaho. We learned
from our mistakes.

And then we applied our knowledge,
sharpening popsicle sticks behind
the gym. Friction was the fire
we started, smoke loping toward
the bus garage. We rubbed it out.

We squeezed our sweaty legs
while she scolded us from her desk.
She talked and talked. We rubbed
her out. We stared out the window
until it was spring.

Friction was in our hands when
we rubbed them together, plotting
revenge. And it was in the rusty
swingset chains we wrapped around
the ringing poles.

Friction made our voices shrill.
Even when we tried to whisper,
it gave us away. And when we rubbed
our papers black, spit
brought them back to life.

# WHERE HAVE THEY GONE?

These were the visionaries of my high school:
the boy who saw a flying saucer
spinning over a soybean field and the girl who ran
her Chevy into a ditch when the image of Jesus
smiled down sadly upon her from a blue Harvestore silo;
otherwise, a normal boy and girl — a track star
and a cheerleader.  He was on the quiet side, but
she was ordinary in every way, consumed
with angora and the different ways you could wear
a boy's class ring.

Who knows what he was doing out in that field
or why the girl suddenly got the urge to go for a drive.
We did everything in groups — less than four was solitude.
Had we known they'd gone off alone,
we might have sent out a search party.

And I'm thinking that miracles will never cease,
that someone will always be flying off
for an overnighter in the Devil's Triangle
or taking telephone calls from Houdini in her teeth.
The boy's saucer spinning like a top
seemed perfectly reasonable (we were only surprised
at its size:  we expected something more commodious
than a dinner plate).  And we all felt so trapped
in our own bodies, so urgent and in heat,
that any extraterrestrial would have been a welcome relief.
Like the story we told at slumber parties,
of the hooked man and lovers' lane,
it took us out of ourselves.

Where have they gone, this boy and girl?
Where have any of us gone?
How long have we been stranded on this earthlike place,
confusing our memories with our dreams?  If I met them
on the street, I wouldn't recognize either one.
In their senior pictures they looked as impassive as wax,
smooth and featureless as spies, passing through a world
that could only fail to charm.
Already they bore no resemblence to the kids
who gave new meaning to swamp gas and clouds,
who lusted so openly for saving grace.

# CINEMA VÉRITÉ

This is an art theatre.
And it's a little like
my old high school gym —
the same wooden seats,
the same sharp scent of mold.
If someone had made a film
of my high school, say
when JFK was killed,
they could show it here
on this sloping screen
(that resembles a trampoline
turned on its side) and
it would be an amazing sight
for there would be such fear
on the faces of so many
watching TV.

Just before it happened
we were watching Carole Worley,
in the last row of sixth
period, open a Nestle's
Crunch with the stiletto
of her fingernail.  I will never
forget how quietly she could
do it.  One of those intercoms
hummed by the door, and just before
the flag tore through the air
there was the murmur of static
as if someone had placed
a hand over the microphone
and was listening.

We never imagined how hard
it would be to sleep, or
how some of us, home on Sunday
morning (because we couldn't stop
watching TV) saw Jack Ruby
stick a gun into Lee Harvey
Oswald's belly, and the way
Oswald caved in, pushing
his mouth out in a silent O.
This would be a part

of what was shown.

Eventually we went numb,
and in our fantasies
the Beatles or Barbra
Streisand took Kennedy's
place. There were nightly
body counts, LBJ and his
scar. Everything we learned
we got from the screen —
condensed, mutilated or redundant,
like this film about the decadence
and banality of everyday life.
It ends with an apocalypse
where a major U.S. city
burns to the ground
and the last thing you see
are the hordes, faces melting,
running into the light.
When Kennedy was president
they were still telling us
that hiding under our desks
would do some good.

# ROCKET ATHLETIC BOOSTERS

Friday nights began when men from
the booster club, guys with big bellies,
climbed a tipsy ladder to the press box
which was really just a couple two-by-
fours over annihilation. They had to
lift themselves like farmers
into a hay mow and pray their thin butts
caught enough board.

They charted scrawny kids whose helmets
rested on their shoulders, who fulfilled
some busy pattern in the half-light.
And in September you could still smell
corn like something spicy
and the whole thing sounded like crickets
gone mad.

But in November the game went like an
ice breaker working the Great Lakes
and the old guys in the press box
hopped carefully back and forth
on their tip toes blowing steam.

# AT THE BOTANICAL GARDENS

A boy, down on his knees,
gazes into his reflection
in the lily pond.  We pause
at the mounted sepia print,
meant to acquaint us with
our fanciful past.  It shows
three women, impossibly
demure, posed on lily pads.

We are headed for the biosphere,
but first we must see
the new Narcissus, this blond
in unlaced high-tops and
cellophaned hair, so thoroughly
absorbed in his own image
that we wonder if he has
conjured up some memory
of a tragic past.

Where the boy kneels
above the echo of his face,
these three once pushed off
like swans, laced into s-curves
of corsets and bustles —
so substantial that if
they had suddenly vanished
their satin dresses could have
stood alone.

As I imagine they have, holding
in their folds some shape
or smell of time.  Here,
where the rolling echo
of jets reminds us
that this is a modern
world, time passes as it
always has, in things
that flower and die.

Even today there is
a wedding in the Japanese

Garden, and beneath our
feet something thick pushes
against the soil, yearning
to be born — as we do,
into a forgiving world.
The boy, bending even lower,
whispers: Remember me.

# SINCERE

The man with the artificial heart
makes plans to go on vacation.
The two sides of his heart
clap together like hooves.

His blood splashes
in a small rubber suitcase.
He has packed for a long journey.
The soul hums contentedly

at home in the vessel
that once held his heart,
displayed on television
looking meaty and a little fat.

He asks the reporter
if she wants to feel.
Her smile skips a beat
and then she grasps the ticking piece

which swings jauntily
at the good man's side.
And just goes to show
how far a man can travel.

# THE MISSING CHILD

The missing child is not
missing within himself.  He is
at war in a place
where nothing is
familiar.

For one day he wanders
a field of corn,
an ocean of parked cars,
or sleeps in a place
where dogs fought.

The voices of those who
are searching ring out
in his dreams.  They
frighten him deeper
into himself.

In town, an old
picture of his face
stares out from every shop
window (his hair much
lighter than it is now).

A solitary child
is brought in, approved,
and the search is called off.

As this happens,
one who is still lost
crawls away from the voice
of a stranger
walking close by
who calls his name softly.

A shadow slides by
in the weeds, but the tall
shoes that hesitate
clearly intend to steal,
not to save.

# NATURAL BORDERS

Our spy has brought back souvenirs — rugs
and a box of fur hats. It takes two of
their people to help him with his bags,
although the clothes he wore when
he was captured have worn out.
They each carry the black briefcases
I have heard they use for lunchboxes.

This is the bridge we use to trade spies —
today, six of theirs for our one flyer,
a lean-jawed man who flew a plane
that for all practical purposes was
invisible. We dare not smile
or show relief — there's a bureaucratic
order to these things. For instance,
we always trade spies just before dawn.

This is how it looks from above, from a
satellite or one of those flat-winged
jets. We've already got the missiles
on film (and those suspicious silver
trailers), not to mention the two dozen
older men facing one another on the bridge,
which only a spy can cross.

The road — what's left of it — has been sealed
to ordinary travelers. Only the airwaves go
where they want — Benny Goodman, for instance,
to show what good lives we lead back home.
In an hour the frantic copy will tick from
the machines, surprising the world that a deal
has been struck (as if we were *allies*).

But for now, everything is subdued,
because this is how we act when we meet
the other side. We wait — we need a referee,
someone to signal when to walk, shake
hands, trade places. And all the while
we face this mystery: their hills,
their trees (they look like oaks),
and the dark water we call a border.

# LE CÔTE D'AZUR

In 1967 I hitchhiked the length of France
with Sharon Martin, a beauty and mercenary.
We spent one night in the Gare de Lyon
and I slept with my head in her lap
while she planned a comeback
in the Miss Ohio Pageant.

That winter she was working on her talent
and her tan.  Late at night, after
too many games of Thumper and chugging
*Panther Pils*, she sang
*You're a Grand Old Flag* in the Plaza
of the Sun God, as if He could help her win.

I helped her shop for the world's smallest
bikini, and in the dressing room noticed
a scar at the top of her hip,
the silvery trellis of a burn
from a household accident that she
wouldn't describe.  And subsequently,
I watched everything tan but that scar,
enchanted by that one ordinary thing.

I helped critique her answers
to the Five Questions and knew Sharon
would never win Miss Congeniality.
She went about it like a shark,
separating blood from water.  She
was the reigning Fourth-Runner-Up
and had learned from her mistakes.

As we lay on the rocky beach at Nice
and fended off vets from a lousy war
and turned methodically every half hour,
she polished her act.  It was like studying
for a test, all psych-out and memorization.
It smelled like something cooking, rocks
punching us in the pelvis, everyone changing clothes
in the open.  It was nothing like up the boulevard
at the Negresco where even the porters
wore plumage from endangered species.

Sharon was a great klepto and we lived
on *Vache Qui Rit* and marmalade.

When she climbed the steps to her plane
I watched her with a judge's eye.
When she waved, I imagined her turning
in a black Jantzen one-piece, a satin sash
rippling between her breasts.

Later, as I sat on the beach, facing
a hazy red sunset, a sun she was already
chasing to America, I watched
each white Caravelle that rose from the airport
as if it were carrying her home.
I had her going all the way to Atlantic City,
belting out patriotic songs, a little flat,
but fervant, clipping out over the dark runway
in her high heels.  I forgot how in the States
beauty is leggy, fixed,
and in abundance.

Afterwards, I heard about a nasty fight
with her college halfback boyfriend
and making some jumpy commercials for Ryan Homes.
And then Sharon disappeared,
like all my old friends, into daily life,
into a job demonstrating gas appliances,
arriving before me at adulthood,
which seemed more like a place
than a time — where no one could follow
or ever find you again.

# THE INITIATE

She has joined the ultimate club.
She can see a wig coming a mile away.
She can feel her own, as unreal
as a bathing cap she wears all the time.
She knows about the trickle of fungus
they drip into her veins — a drug so powerful
they wear masks to handle the syringe. She's
just glad they haven't put a zipper
in her side. It's not so bad, after all —

There's one younger than herself
with children who need raising.
Too poor for a wig, she wears a headscarf,
skin tight, and her brow is as pink
and wrinkled as a baby's. They smile
and compare notes like a grisly comedy
team, or listen while the barber tells
how he got discouraged and went fishing
for a week. Now he bubbles into a bag
and fears he jinxed himself.

*Obey the doctor* he warns.
This man's like the kiss of death,
the one who doesn't play fair —
who talks about failure and
grows more translucent every week.
They recline in their space chairs
like astronauts sailing to a new star.
The chemo is timeless, a warp.
When she wakes up, she's lost a day
and her insides are glass.

It is easy to forget how to get home,
or exactly what it means *to go home*.
So much easier in this half-light
to slip from the careless arms of gravity,
to fall into space, which awaits her,
and all of us, whether we join this club or not.

# GETTING THERE

When I drive to see you
I know I am getting close
when I see the Red Cross planes
circling the Air Force base.

I am twenty miles away,
driving downhill,
past the white radar
and the dark red barn.

Sometimes a fighter
tears through the sky,
fire burning in its hollow core.
Once an olive-drab transport
paddled downwind, and
dropped a package into the woods.

I imagine the city beyond,
gleaming white — beyond the flood
plain, the bridges, and
the big limestone downtown.
All that empty now, on a Sunday,
a day that smells sweet,
almost palpably of rainwater
and grass.

But, before I can get there
shadows of big, low planes
flash over my car
like fish.  And I try
to keep them in sight,
imagining the vast dark emptiness
of the sky they displace.

# SILENT RUN

It takes place with such leisure — the ambulance
gliding to a stop across the street, the lazy flow
of red lights. If it weren't for the short wave radios
we wouldn't know a thing about this neighborhood.

The stretcher stands abandoned on the front lawn,
as spotless as a shrine, and more people enter the house
than come out. With the doors open we can almost guess
what it would be like to ride away in such a thing, to be
so *celebrated*. Once through an open door we saw a man,
swaddled to the waist and strapped in, combing his hair.
Today it looks just like a kitchen — a galley in outer space.

It's always on a spring day like this, a moist salad
of wild onions and dandelions in the air, and mowers whining
as they will now until November. A baseball game
murmurs from a car being waxed — it's a soothing ritual,
like a dream, part of what happens when someone dies.

Sometimes it's just like a social call, and they leave
without taking a thing, as if all those people have been
delegated to check up on you, to remind you
that even on a day like this they will come,
in no particular hurry — polite, almost silent,
as if they have known all along when it's your time,
your turn to take this long ride.

# PART TWO — DOMESTIC SCIENCE

# THE CHANGELINGS

We dig into the knuckles of dead roses
and the old roots tear like fabric.  I stand
on the shoulders of the spade, as if I've found
a crow's nest stabbed into the sod, but
the horizon rolls empty to the palisades.

We have a whole barn of horse manure,
and we're spooning it under, still hot,
like a pair of nursemaids feeding the soil,
feeding the healthy roots and the new ones that
came in the mail, a half dozen green sticks,
named after couturiers, queens and movie stars.

You almost expect them to walk away on their
spiny cane legs, rustling in their shrinkwrap,
showing off designer labels.  They look like
something that came from the Late Show:
a new, thornier *Day of the Triffids.*
I will call them by name as I urge them to grow,
breathing softly into their sweet open mouths.

When the spade's flat head chomps into roots
I feel it in my own gristle.  And you're whistling
some shapeless tune, completely at rest,
even though we're working hard, packing dirt
around these misshapen canes — the survivors that
rode out winter in a place unfit for roses,
where the sour lake winds have even the horses
kicking the sides of their stalls, where every spring
something dead goes back into the ground,
and the soil, richer here than anywhere else
on the farm, is cut and folded, as if
cookery were taking place on some grand scale.

Here roses will bloom for at least one season
and shine in the evening light the way some rocks,
split open and still warm from lying in the sun,
bear crystals in their dark, secret hearts.

# EYES

The man next door can move earth
or push down trees with one of his yellow
machines. The trunks pop open,
jagged and unseemly.
His three grey cats follow him.
They are intensely shy of everything
but the man. They walk out over the snow,
testing each foot before stepping.
One is mottled. Orange calico
touches it lightly like a suntan.
In January, when the man towed my car
out of Lipe's orchard, the cats watched
over their shoulders. Their tails lay
like extra animals on the snow.
Set back on the road again, I paid the man,
handing warm dollar bills up to the cab.
The cats had already started home,
single file, low, running
in the tracks made by the machine.
I can only imagine what it would be like
having those cats run at me,
crying out, tails aloft, licking my hands
with dry, serrated tongues.

# BUTCHER

Every once in awhile a milkfed calf goes down the road
in the back of a pickup. He vanishes over the hill
looking sleepy and a little surprised at the rush.
Sometimes, it's a big red hog, braced and insulted
in a bouncy wooden trailer, and the farmer driving
with both hands on the wheel, already smiling at
the thought of ready cash. I have lived here
long enough to be almost soothed by this ritual:
first the pickups, and then the refrigerator trucks
speeding past on their way to the meat locker.
And then there is a pause — nothing else as noisy
or fast happens for the rest of the morning.
It gets so quiet you can almost hear the jays
gliding swiftly into the hearts of trees,
or the soil ticking, merely breathing out the damp.
On the way home, the farmer, empty in back, lightened,
will drive by with one elbow out the window,
radio blasting a song like *Lucille*, and, if you wave,
he'll wiggle all the fingers he's got left.

# RED

In snapshots dogs have red eyes.
They glow out from the pictures
more sorrowful than mad.
You wish you had red hair
and in some photographs you do —
an out-of-focus magenta fuzz
that reminds me of some blond
men: When they grow beards
their whiskers come in wiry
and maroon.

I have always thought
of red hair as a sport
(like the single ear of Indian
corn in the field of relentlessly
engineered hybrids)
and that all redheads must feel
partly freak. I recall my
grandmother leaning into the car
and saying to my cherry-headed
cousin Marge, *My Land!*
*Your skin is as white as milk!*

You believe wanting something
will make it so. No one wants
the hair they have.

# THE WINDING SHEET

A spider with the gall of Christo
is sewing my house to the ground.
It rides a guy wire of spit
from the west eaves to the marigolds.

And back up, as if its gory ribbon
were pneumatic.  I can't see its eyes
or where it looks — perhaps at me,
gauging the length of rope it would take
to haul in so much protein.

It skates the geometry of hunger,
a thing of such appalling beauty
that I know people who push the Hoover
furiously into every corner, convinced
of a spider wherever two angles meet.

Ever since this morning
a grasshopper has been spinning
in the interstices of silk and oblivion,
legs pummeling web into its own lopsided shroud.

The spider, calmly ignoring its prey,
swings down a thread just pulled
from its gut, stitching my house
into the hem of this impossible design.

# THE FAITHFUL ONE

The steers, five cousins, stand hip deep
in the green water of that forlorn crater
at the pasture's edge. It's not one of
those square ponds left by the Interstate,
but a farm pond so old no one remembers
how it got there — surely not the steers
who have a half-life of one year (you can
hear the bawling some mornings as the pickups
race down the road to the butcher).

The dog is hightailing it for the water.
It's hard to tell if she wants to join or
torment the five steers, spotted like her,
but with tails they can use to smash flies.
They move like the world's slowest choral
dance team — one foot forward — deeper into
the oily water. They do everything together,
even chew. The hound, looking joyous to see
them, tosses her head, her loose pinto ears,
and prances down to the rocky shore.

Whatever she's up to they don't care —
you can see it in their rolling, bored eyes.
The dog, who some days can run between
their legs for ten minutes before
she gets the picture, never feels jilted.
She's never going to let those five dampen
her optimism. Some day those steers will
see the light, and run with her to the woods,
filling like so many rawhide balloons,
and help her chase those crazy birds.

# NIGHT THOUGHTS

You have more patience than me.
You have seen more stars fall.
Some of the stars, you point out,
have been dead for thousands
of years.  Parts of constellations
could be missing, or imploded —

a thought so depressing
I'd rather watch the winglights
of a tiny plane, sawing
on the diagonal, low over our land.
It will cross our place, then
Ginther's, then sink
onto the packed turf of the county airport
and roll toward the crop dusters.

I'd rather not think of stars
belonging to anyone, like our sun.
Or making part of a shape,
like a dipper, or bear.  I believe
in the high-strung metal and gyro
that go with the lights overhead.
But I can't believe in the calm face inside,
lit with green, reading the lights below,
like stars.

The death of a star is too big.
And a falling star isn't really
a star.  When I look at a contrail,
suspended and spreading,
I don't see people serving cocktails
or reading the New York *Times*.
I see something too heavy to float.
And when I see stars,
I see ice.

# VERNAL

It seems like all life is being squeezed flat
on the road to Boskydell — box turtles,
a tiny aqua snake, a fat crustacean that
must have crawled up from the primal kitchen.

Every morning now there is a possum
dead and swollen beside the road, and
I remember the small bloodshot eyes
I surprised once in the garage. I
thought how easy it would be to kill
an animal that defends itself
by pretending to be dead.

This must be the planet's way
of preventing overpopulation —
instilling in the road an irresistable
allure:  smooth heat-retaining
asphalt, level bed of the cold-blooded.
It's the big dinner plate of spilled
grain, rotten fruit, and the half-
eaten Whopper — exotic as a baited hook.

When I run to Boskydell I know
how easily I could become as splayed
as the frogs that peel from the tar
like labels.  I ride my bike past
the horse farm, and a young rabbit bolts
from the safety of the ditch into
my spokes.  I veer into the path
of a speeding Monte Carlo and barely
avoid being thrown into the waving cattails.

At the top of the hill the white grin
of a possum is a playground for flies.
Even when this possum is a piece of ragged
leather, or only a grease mark for the
collie P. C. to nuzzle, the miraculous
creature in the woods gives birth
to fourteen more — three too many
for her eleven teats.  The eleven
will taste in her milk this passion

for the road. Their red eyes already
smolder for that narrow strip,
which even now teems with life.

# PILGRIMS

You could tear off a piece of road
and chew it like Black Jack gum
the day we went to the junkyard —
past Slaughterpen Road, past Fuquay -
Varina, farther south than we'd ever
been — to buy a seatbelt for the Maverick.

Hubcaps were piled around the gate
like prostheses at some Catholic
shrines.  The nuclear family in the
office showed us on the chart
where to find the Fords, then
the youngest son opened the back
door and pointed us down an alley
of calamity and shattered glass.

The geckos raced from us like skinny
hens, and we followed their flail
tracks through the pink dust
to the Mustangs, Pintos, and LTDs.
If Henry Ford could have seen it,
he would have worked harder
on the soybean car.

Every car we had ever known was there:
the Corvair, smooth as a kidney bean,
the cruel El Camino, the last Rambler —
and all the family sedans that went crazy
at the crossroads and the EMS
came running with the Jaws of Life.

They all looked as if they had been
thrown, or dropped from great heights.
Tires were torn, filled with black
water and breeding mosquitoes.
The smell of sex was as strong
as the smell of death.  Weeds grew
through the cracked vinyl seats,
up through the festive combs
and parts of sunglasses.  And
there were black pennies that
no one would spend or ever save.

The sun went dark, the way it gets
in an eclipse — brown, and bright
at the edges — and the air smelled old,
greasy like the coveralls that hung
for years on the basement hook.
Oil soaked into the red dirt, and I
sat, right there in Kentucky,
head between my knees, watching
the ground come up, braced to survive
any crash — no belt cinching me
to the fragile structure of life.

# EIGHT COWS

*Sometimes I would like to*
*forget all this, buy a small farm*
*and take care of eight cows*
                    — a victim of burnout

What would I do without you?
You have reminded me of cows,
their awkward shapes in which
they seem so terrifyingly to float.
You have reminded me of the cows
of my childhood.  The steaming
barn in the dark morning,
the soft crunching of the straw,
a large eye rolling while my father
emptied the udders, while I poked
at the hide trying to figure out
what it was that it was stretched
over.  Surely not flesh,
not blood and nerves, but something
like milk, before it becomes milk,
small cows in small barns.

I can hardly drive through the countryside
without pulling up at the dairy
farms, staring out at the fields
as if cows were relics
of a lost past.  The brindle cow
who lies on her side, will she
ever get to her feet again?  The mystery
of the four stomachs, the cud,
the cow flops I once followed
to the river when I was six
and we hadn't raised cows
for a year.  If you look away
from a cow, she grows invisible,
becoming part thistle, part cloud.
When cows gallop to the barn at night
they fill like sails, dewlaps swinging,
a fleet of good girls, coming home
across the fluttering bay.

# PART THREE — MUSIC OF THE SPHERES

# FISH HANDS

The mechanic's son
can fix a Betsy
in his sleep.  Raw bones
drag his coveralls
after him like
shed skin.

Pa tells how
he cut his teeth
on a retread.  There is
no way he can get
his buttons closed
over those wrench
wrists.

Hump back,
sight fixed on
a purring V-8, he has
a vestigial memory
of the first Dyna-Flo
blasting down the drag
like a boat.

Rush hour,
music of the spheres.
He washes down
lunch with a hose,
inseparable from the
glaucous light
of the bay.

Cocked,
and poised for another
sound — an engine skips.
His heart flies out
to the Bonneville
breaking water
at the light.

# LES DEUX PAULETTES

The gulf trembles like an orange cut open
Pelicans glide silently as pitchers from spar buoy
    to spar buoy
The sun is a red lip about to be eaten
Les deux Paulettes stretch their toes and lay back as they do
    every night to watch — this spectacle, this dream
Les deux Paulettes who love one another like sisters
Lizards lay thickly as dogs, panting beneath their chairs,
    bright eyes hovering like intelligent marbles
    locked on the last point of light
Les deux Paulettes have a name for it, *Tomato Baby*
And the night, *a box for the stars, a mirror for the moon*
They watch the bay take light like a necklace,
    strand by strand
They watch the water pull away turgid as ink
Their arms fall in ivory arcs upon their hair, their throats,
    smoothing their soft, folding laps
The lightkeeper's signal starts up with a tortured whine
The first rotation claps like foil off the sand
Les deux Paulettes say to each other, *C'est incroyable.*
    *Chaque jour la même chose.*
A lizard curls and dreams of the sun, a pinhole burning
    phosphor into its wet, spurting heart

# GUM FOR BREAKFAST

Basketballs thump the playground
I am not close enough
but I can hear the screech of
Pro-Keds      grab cement
and my hands get
a little dirty      Girls at recess
race like banners
at the edge of a field
A bell rings      and brick
red balls roll down
hill      My hands
are a little callused
from skin      the cat
There is never time
to drink      enough
A wad      of gum
indented with teeth
grins in the water
fountain      I'm still
breathing heavy

# BEGINNING PERSPECTIVE

In drawings by children
the chicken looms over the house
the sun weeps
and all hands are mittens

little men bask
in the glorious bird's
shadow
its shoulders move like the clouds
muscled layer beneath feather

a tiny girl stands
in the doorway of her house
eyes pinwheeling
looking everywhere but the obvious

finding all things
in their proportion
larger than she
a white sky
blue clouds
a man with the comb of a rooster

and through the door
where the tiny girl lives
is darkness
unimagined

# THE WORD

I stared at *October* so long
I was sure it couldn't be spelled
with an *O*.  I thought about words
until I knew I'd gone insane.
The prairie thundered with buffalo.
Why not bison?  How can the range
be a stove and the prairie too?
Until I was twenty-one
I thought I knew how to spell,
but then the sudden configuration
of a word made my head spin.

The Chinese draw a tree,
then the sun,
and finally a man standing
with his head in the sun.
They don't have to know
how to spell, only to draw
and hold the pictures
of the ten kingdoms
palpable and complete
in the silken darkness
of the mind, the way
a magician's scarf
conceals an endless supply
of white doves.

# THE INCREDIBLE JOURNEY

The two kids next door
go by wearing clothes
you can almost see
being outgrown.  The girl
carries a basketball
like an orb.  The boy,
his books in a Foodtown
bag.  They walk

like they are royalty,
or dreaming.  And then,
the fog swallows them,
but you can still hear
the school bells
chime like buoys
in the mist, and
you know they arrived safely
when, after the last bell,
they reappear,
carrying their books
like trays, and
a carefully worn emptiness
in their eyes.

# THE MECCA COURT & GRILL

The postcard shows a place as flat
and uninhabited as a movie set,
tourist cabins for those who have lost their way.
It is out of context, the way putt-putts
or water slides suddenly rear up
out of a cornfield at the edge of town,
and you never notice because
there isn't a person on earth who goes there anymore.

This reminder of a place I have never longed for
came in the mail this morning, along with
another card, titled *Desert Plants of the Southwest.*
An idealized landscape, it shows one of everything:
one Yucca, a Joshua tree, Mescal, Buckhorn,
Ocatillo — as if the desert had been planted
by an ambitious, but finicky gardener.

It would be like God sending a postcard of Earth
to the seraphim, showing two of everything
patiently boarding a rickity Ark: *Wish you were here:
Only evil continually.*

I have a postcard of the Jackalope,
surely a form of evil. And the Wheat Bell
from someplace in Kansas, and a bunch of cards
I can put my nose through and wear as masks.

I prefer the postcards of my great-grandfather's day,
pictures of real people, like the one of all the Haucks
waiting at Customs in Tijuana, clad in raccoon coats,
Homburgs, saddle shoes, and carrying piñatas,
as if headed for an exotic football game.

Or the one of the great-aunts in their white
summer dresses, lounging on the porch steps
like the Caryatids at rest. Even though they are young
they stare into the camera like old women, tired
and a little angry, as if the photograph
were a form of death.

It is like going to the cemetery
where the headstones of Piermans fill a country acre,
but not feeling any connection, or fear,
even though I see myself in their eyes.

# ZOMBIE

There is always one of her
floating into sight
as if borne on an electric wire.
She dances on the crosstown bus,
but only when it is in motion.

She wears a bandana
over her mouth and clicks
like a geiger counter.
On the hottest day
she wraps herself in wool.

The crowds part before her
but you can't avoid it.
She meets you at the top
of the subway stairs
and screams into your face:

> *If only I had a blackboard*
> *I could describe every form of illness*
> *in this city!* Her fevered breath roars
> at you like something you ate long ago.

What is that halo of static?
This lingering aura of ozone?
Can it arc from her
to you (this slow
but certain murder)?

Your blood freezes
as if scrubbed in a freon bath.
One touch from her would either
heal or send you shimmying
over the platform edge,
crooning your love
to the crazy third rail.

# NOVA

Birds the color of grass
shake themselves from the lawn
and fly through my window

It is not as cold
as it can get
but the earth has turned
sullen and the skies
are dragged southward

Any night
the only color is sodium,
the fastening down of darkness
like a clamp

It is impossible to talk of it
but beneath every conversation
is a listening.  If we relax

water will pound our land
into shards

At the continent's core
we hear a shifting, streams
helpless to meet the sea

Nothing can be done about
this attraction, or how
we have to force ourselves
not to watch the sky

Our worst dream is a lifeboat
rudderless on the North Atlantic
filled to overflowing,
dying in the salt spray
and cold

We will do no better
when faced with ice
rolling down from the north
like a tongue

Tokens gathered around us
we will have to live together,
human voices will sing
higher than the wolves

# PART FOUR — THE AGE OF KRYPTON

# HEARING HARRY SAY

I am astride Jim's
shoulders, and there is Bess,
and now Margaret Truman,
and they are hugged
to Harry's side
by the black wings
of his overcoat.
This is the presidential
portrait: Harry
Truman whistle stopping
through Ottawa, Ohio,
October 11, 1948.
His train, the Magellan,
steams at the old
Rex Theatre siding.
Beneath the marquee a
small crowd of citizens
keeps a respectful
distance from the platform
(which most days is a loading
dock for the mill across
the street). Microphones
bristle like a bouquet of
cattails and electric
razors. Truman says
what he always does
and Bess is Boss once
more. He squeezes her
to his side and someone
below me, hunting cap
pushed back over red
ears mutters, let's hope
Margaret doesn't sing.
The train barely stops
rolling and Harry disappears
over the Blanchard River,
receding, growing smaller,
until three white faces
glow in an autumn
setting, pale ovals
floating over black wool

coats, and the crowd
balances on silver rails,
waves goodbye —
*goodbye Harry goodbye* —
as if in that short time
he became one of us,
part uncle, part vestigial
memory of FDR.
And somehow we find
our way back to the truck
parked on a side street
where yellow leaves rattle
up and down the curb,
but we are still
watching for Harry
one last time as the black
butt of the train rocks and
groans down the narrow
country easement — the
Nickle Plate — toward Lima
or Dayton, into an election
no one expects the man to win.
And so when the train
vanishes — simply becomes
a point too small to see —
and all that's left is
something humming, like
the strings of a piano
after the last long
note, we will remember
one time we heard
what Harry had to say.

# THE APPOINTMENT

I will never forget *Onionhead*,
the first movie I ever saw,
in Toledo, at the Paramount.
I went with my grandfather
and we sat in the balcony
as far back as we could go.

The show had already started
so we crept in the dark
toward a seat, and I remember turning
and seeing Andy Griffith's big face,
khaki colored and grinning.
We felt our way toward the sound
of sprockets and the fiery window
above the last row.

Cigarette smoke toppled
in the floating air. Dust
sizzled into the vast
canopy. Between me and the screen
was a man's bald head and
the smell of popcorn being chewed.
I didn't know why my grandmother
had to come all the way to Toledo
for the dentist, or that she was losing
her teeth, one by one. All I knew
was the sea sound of the theatre
and the frosted lamps that glowed
like dim rainbows along the wall.

We left before the show ended,
crawling back over the shuttle of knees,
so I must have imagined the man
at the Wurlitzer, playing like Captain Nemo.
I must have imagined that I slept
because I remember the white hands
moving in the dark so well.

# POLIO SUMMER

It wasn't the disease
that worried.  It was the apparatus:
Iron Lung.  Quarantine.
The first I became aware of it
were signs in the windows
on Old Main Cross Street
and a hanging silence
even in the cars
that drove slowly home from work.

And even though the shades were drawn
I felt watched.
That was Quarantine.
I imagined a girl
like myself
in bed in a high dark room
losing touch with her friends
and the feeling in her legs.

And I remember the dark
flickering quality of the Sister Kenney ads
and the small March of Dimes children
quavering in metal braces,
diminished by the metal.

I hurried through my piano lessons,
and Mother walked me home
to protect me from the children
carelessly allowed outside to play.
On that empty street in Findlay
on a yellow August day
I felt the iron lung in my heart,
pulling, pulling for cold air.

And soon after, they reopened the public
pools, and there was a teacher
who walked around her shortened leg
like a pivot, and a series of visits
from the soldierly school health nurse
who administered the pink shots.

But some stayed in the iron lung
and wrote their answers
with their teeth.

# SEEN IN THE BLUE
# FLUTTERING LIKE AN OLD MOVIE

It was the age of Krypton
and anyone could have their feet
x-rayed. Even Gmeiner's
had a nickleodeon-sized x-ray
machine. And there were my bones —
narrow, wing-like things.

There was a place for me to look
and the woman to look. And then
I got shoes — open-toed Mary Janes
that turned my winged-foot,
fluttering bones into leathery webs.

The sun cooked the curb
where I waited for the light.
Then I crashed across the street
slapping my new shoes. My toes
developed picture-perfect,
only they tingle
and tick like a clock.

# THE PANDORA DRY GOODS

There are buffalo on the road to St. Louis
but the dry goods store is vanishing —
Gregg's, The Leader, Vicki's Shopping Centre,
and even the Pandora Dry Goods where
I bought my gym suits and summer band
uniform.  They are memories like the gurgle
of pneumatic tubes coughing up change
behind the counter.

It always starts the same way — when a store
begins to fail the merchandise becomes so
peculiar that you can hear your own footsteps
yearning for the door.  You expect to see
Rod Serling hovering in the lingerie.
I remember one business run by a family
of ghosts, sad things so eager to please
they frightened their customers away.
The first floor smelled of Ambush and ammonia.

And there was Patterson's with the eternal
Boy Scout uniform display on the mezzanine
and the choice between a listing circular
staircase and a sinking elevator driven by
a sly man on a jump seat, jiggling
a joy stick between his knees.

My prom dress from Ann Francis still hangs
in a closet in Ottawa, Ohio.  I remember the day
a car plunged through the front window,
crushing pedestrians into a mannequin's pink
arms, and the blood sliding down
the back of the umbrella display while a rigid
woman tried on gloves.  That was the beginning.

Or did the dry goods begin to fail
when women stopped wearing high heels
and gloves to shop?  I haven't carried a purse
in years, but I can see Helen of Pandora Dry
Goods as if it were yesterday — Helen with
the soft black moustache and sturdy
Enna Jetticks, arranging Red Wing boots

on the basement steps. She would
come up behind you like Dracula and whisper,
*May I help you*, when all you wanted
was to meet your grandmother outside,
or in the park, or never again.

Bad luck didn't kill the merchant
class. Not even the May Company or
Federated Stores. It was a clerk standing
all day alone, folding the same stack
of underwear, trying not to listen for
the door. Right up to the end, Vicki
of Vicki's Shopping Centre spent the whole
day on the phone talking to the invisible
psychotherapist. And Uncle Carl
set fires in small appliances.

Bad buying affects the mind — all those
butte knits and Red Cross shoes
collecting dust season after season.
Pop beads and too many kilt pins left
in Notions. Now I no longer fear
the tall thin woman in charge of brassieres.
I drive to the anonymity of the mall
and stand in line at a Service Desk.
But I still listen for the swift approach
of the lunatic clerk who will not
be denied. My heart longs for
the soft intrusion of a revolving door.

# PUBLIC HEALTH

The young have no sense of policy,
therefore, vaccinations always came
as a surprise. We lined up
for everything, and no one suspected
the cold needles glistening in rows
until the gym doors swung open
and an ether of cotton soaked in alcohol
poured out. We bucked and
the line began to implode. A name
pinnacled from the ceiling: *Mrs. Mann,*
*Mrs. Mann.* The county health nurse.
There was only enough time for
the Methodists to claim her,
to brag that she sang every Sunday
in choir. Some of us couldn't
believe her out of the blue pincord
uniform or the white hose that stretched
over her long and boardlike calves.
We aimed our anger at the Methodists
and watched them snake up to the table
rolling their sleeves over impossibly
bony arms. Our eyes avoided the needles
laid out on towels and the vials of clear
vaccine, steaming from the freezer
like jiggers of Russian vodka.
All this glimmered in the half-light
of the gym where some of us forgot
to breathe and fell like logs, eyes
rolling into whiteness. Some people
sat for a few minutes in the bleachers,
dazed and holding gauze to their shoulders.
The rest of us sniggered back to our rooms
butting each other in the arms,
pinching the smart but clumsy girl
who had the shot in her hip.
Is it any wonder that we howled
instead of sang, or that we couldn't
settle down for the spelling bee?
There was no sense of having been
spared a shriveled leg or death from
preposterous disease. There was only

the uneasy sense of Mrs. Mann
who was dark and efficient
and who seemed to know each one of us
by name. She raised my arm,
swabbed, pinched up enough skin
to sink the needle home.
I carried my arm from the gym
like a doll I would bed down in a box,
stiff and throbbing with fever.

# XMAS

I can see my childhood bedroom
just as it was, my old toys still
scattered on the floor; and smell —
almost taste — the pungent odor of
Lincoln Logs and Davy Crockett coonskin
cap. Sometimes there are my sisters'
newer toys: Etcha-Sketch, Creepy
Crawlers, and one Barbie with tits
that could put out your eyes.

I think of everything as mine,
that things will always be as I remember,
even my old grade school, torn down
for a new building in 1955.
In my mind, both schools stand
on the same spot — the blackened fire escapes
hanging from the newer upstairs windows.

There are still toys that I want:
I want one of those long, low metal cars
that shoots sparks when you give it a push,
robots that run by remote control,
or any Howdy Doody item.

I want to walk into my old school
pulling Flubadub on a string, listening
for the wood floor's creak as we pass
down the dark hall to second grade.
I'd like to be back in that room
with cocoons hatching in the cloakroom,
the sink smelling of finger paint and paste.

I'd like to be back in my bedroom,
down on my knees in front of some toy,
cold air seeping in at the window,
everything quiet after presents are opened,
something going on, but I don't know what.
I'd change the track on my Lionel set.
I'd have *more* track, a bridge,
a few mountains. And a station
where a bunch of plastic people stand

eternally in groups awaiting departure.

Or go back in time even further,
to the night before, to all the gifts still
stacked beneath the tree, lights bubbling,
tinsel shimmering as if some invisible wind
were blowing through the house. I would lift each box
and gently shake it, reverent and convinced
of a Santa Claus wrestling a rocking
horse through outer space, intent on
its blessed passing through the chimney.

# ABSENT

Each time we passed her house
on the back road to town, Father said,
Poor little Doris Maxine. I barely recalled
my old classmate who, in second grade,
moved to a new school district,
into a white rambling farmhouse
with curlicues of gingerbread at the roof
and a porch wide enough to skate on.

After awhile I only remembered her pale,
almost pink hair, and that she was the first
of us to need glasses, thick ones
with baby blue frames. There wasn't much else
to set her apart: we all wore smocked dresses,
colored too hard, and, between recesses,
sweated and stuck to the screeching wooden chairs,
unaware of the miracle that transformed us
into readers and counters.

The next year, when Doris Maxine didn't come back,
we gave her place to Betsy Baker, the new doctor's
daughter, who was blond, sang loud,
and wore taps on her patent leather shoes.
We forgot the Agner girl until she died.
A fluke, Mother said, a child so young
dying of stroke.

And the back road rises to a cemetery
of bleached white tablet stones. They lean
against the wind, as if gravity, not vandals
were pulling them down. The new graves
are in the back, so you can't see the obelisk
for the first of us to die — the one who left,
was forgotten, and then drowned in her own red blood,

Teaching us that this is how it always happens —
when no one is thinking of you,
or could even imagine how you reeled around outside,
near the grape arbor, pulling down vines,
dragging against the trellis,
hanging on for dear life, trying to fathom
this earthquake, this tremor.